Love Lives Here

Andi Ellis-Smith

This book is dedicated to my family, unique and special.

I love you

x

In a town where the sun shines so bright,
Live families of every shape and size, what a beautiful sight!

Some have a Mum and a Dad by their side,
In every achievement, they show their pride.

Some have two mums who paint skies full of stars,
And love their children, for who they are

Some have two Dads who read
the bedtime story,
Who celebrate the small wins
and share in all their glory.

Some kids live with Grandparents,
they're so kind and wise,
Who teach about times gone by
and, whose love you cannot deny.

Some children live with one parent, or live across two. That's okay, their loves is always with you.

Some children stay with foster families when help is needed, With loved ones who support and give power to succeed.

Some kids have siblings, some have none,
Some love reading, and some love to run!

Some families are made of many different races,
With beautiful eyes and bright smiling faces,

Some families have pets, a different kind of friend who brings joy, Always a comfort, as long as you get them a toy!

Some families are built through adoption, with hearts open wide,
Where stories are shared and adventures collide.

Our skin, our hair, the foods we eat,
Bring stories and cultures, that make us complete.

In every home, no matter the name,
The most important thing is love,
that's always the same.

So whether your family is big or it's small,
Different or the same, there's room for us all.

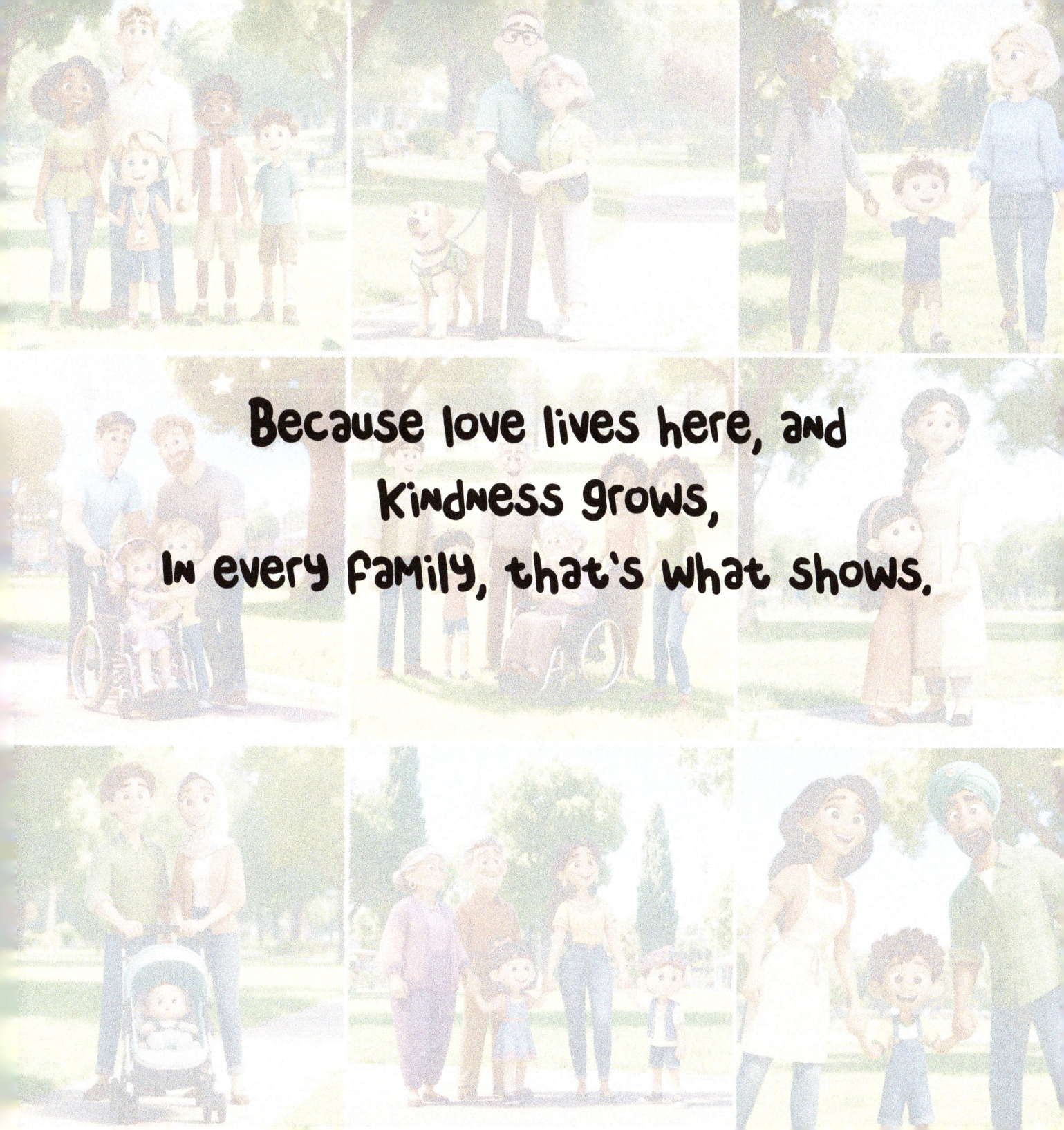

Because love lives here, and kindness grows,
In every family, that's what shows.

David Ribi - Presenter of Milkshake - Channel 5

No two families are the same, and this beautiful book by Andi Ellis-Smith lets us know just how special that is. As I sat down to read it, I couldn't help but think that this is the perfect way to teach our little ones that 'the most important thing is love, and that's always the same.'

A heart-warming message from a very warm-hearted author.

www.instagram.com/ribsy87

Nikki Saunders - Author & Creator of Ready Eddie Go!

When a child recognises their own world on the page, it sends a powerful message. Love Lives Here is a celebration of the beautifully diverse ways families are formed and the many places love can grow. At a time when many children still struggle to see their own lives reflected in character and the stories they read, this book offers a joyful reminder that every family is valid, every child belongs, and love looks wonderfully different from home to home. Love Lives Here makes space for children who are too often left out of traditional narratives.

www.readyeddiego.com
www.nrsaunders.com

About the Author

ANDI ELLIS-SMITH

Andi is the creator behind the social media platforms Dadda & Daddy.

Prior to becoming a parent, Andi has a background of working in schools and in the Local Authority.

Since adopting their first child in 2018, Andi has worked tirelessly to advocate for Adoption, Special Educational Needs and Disabilities (SEND), and LGBTQ+ parents. He does this through his social media platforms, speaking at national events, and giving input to research for projects and policies. Andi has also provided support for SEND children and families across the UK and for those who wish to become parents via adoption.

The family were also regular contributors to the BBC Tiny Happy People channel, sharing their everyday life, whether through practical tips and advice as SEND parents, a same sex parent family or through light-hearted comedy sketches designed to help other parents feel seen, supported, and less alone.

Andi believes that representation in stories is vital for meaningful inclusion. He wanted to create a book in which children and families could see themselves reflected. This is something he wished had existed when he first became a parent. His hope is that this book finds its way into every school library and every home, offering comfort, inclusion, and visibility for all families.

At the heart of everything Andi does has a simple message: it doesn't matter who you are or what your family looks like, whoever you are, all that truly matters is love, in whatever form.

THE END

www.ingramcontent.com/pod-product-compliance
Lightning Source LLC
Chambersburg PA
CBHW061129070526
44584CB00033B/4271